Sulcata Tort

Handbook f(

Detailed Guide on How to

Effectively Raise Sulcata Tortoise

as Pets & Other Purposes;

Includes Its Care& Diseases;

Feeding; Choosing a Breed; Its

Home & So On

By

Markus J. Muench

Copyright@2020

TABLE OF CONTENTS

CHAPTER ONE

INTRODUCTION

The sulcata turtle (Geochelone sulcata), otherwise called the African prodded turtle, is one of the biggest turtle species on the planet. It has an earthy color to yellow shell and thick, yellowish-earthy colored skin, alongside pointed scales— or spikes—on its legs. Local to parched and semiarid districts of Africa, these turtles can adjust to different day to day environments, which is one motivation behind why they have gotten well known as a pet. In any case, they don't make ideal pets for everybody because of their long life expectancies and explicit consideration prerequisites.

Be that as it may, in the event that you can keep them glad and solid, they can make for no particular reason, inquisitive, and benevolent allies.

Species outline

Normal names: Sulcata turtle, African prodded turtle

Logical name: Geochelone sulcata

Grown-up size: 24 to 30 inches in length, gauging 80 to 110 pounds

Future: 70 years or more

Again, the Sulcata Tortoise is the most famous pet turtle on the planet.

Otherwise called African Spurred tortoises they are adored for their special characters – many state they act like canines.

In the event that you need a turtle with a fun and gallant character, at that point look no further.

Sulcata Tortoises can be housed inside or outside. Be that as it may, when they arrive at their grown-up size of 100 pounds, they will require an extremely huge fenced in area to wander, brush and burrow.

Our consideration manage beneath will plot the stuff to raise a solid and glad Sulcata, how to set up their nook, what to take care of them and great cultivation rehearses.

This turtle starts from the deserts of Africa.

The Sulcata Tortoise is a very famous pet and is known for its colossal size, tan and earthy colored shell, and enormous scopes.

Before receiving a child it is ideal to chat with nearby pet shops and re-home a senior as there is an overabundance of Sulcatas around the world.

They make extraordinary pets for first time reptile proprietors who are prepared for a deep rooted responsibility. They can survive beyond 100 years.

Ordinarily they are lone pets and flourish in bondage when brought up in zones that are hot and dry all year. Southern states like Texas are ideal.

On account of their colossal size they should be housed outside – recollect that they are enthusiastic diggers before releasing one in your lawn!

The next chapters will reveal all you need to know regarding sulcata tortoise! Happy perusal!

CHAPTER TWO

SULCATA TORTOISE CONDUCT, TEMPERAMENT, AND HOW TO HOUSE IT PLUS ITS ENVIRONMENT

Sulcata turtles hush up like every single other turtle, and they are enormous and moderate. They likewise will in general be interested animals, once in a while to their drawback. They can without much of a stretch stall out in spaces that are excessively little for them, just as flip themselves over and be not able to right themselves. As pets, these turtles are commonly wonderful and accommodating. They're seldom forceful or regional. In any case, they actually ought not to be dealt with routinely, particularly when they're more youthful and more fragile. Excessive taking care of can pressure a turtle and lead to medical problems or even sudden passing.

Lodging the Sulcata Tortoise

Admittance to an extensive open air fenced in area is ideal for these huge turtles. They need a solid fence that is around 2 feet tall. Furthermore, on the grounds that they tunnel very well, the fence ought to be broadened underground in any event a foot in an outside enclosure. A shelter as a doghouse or little shed is a smart thought to give insurance from the components. What's more, a sloppy flounder might be incorporated for your turtle to splash and poo in.

Lodging grown-up sulcata turtles inside can be unrealistic because of their size. In any case, you should furnish them with a warm space on the off chance that you live in a colder atmosphere. An open air warmed shed or nursery where they can live when it is cool outside can be a reasonable alternative. In the event that you do decide to bring a grown-up sulcata inside, you probably should devote a space to it.

Warmth

Sulcata turtles need hot temperatures to remain solid and dynamic. They can deal with open air temperatures of 100 degrees Fahrenheit or higher as long as they approach an obscure spot where they can go in the event that they have to cool off. If the evening temperature dips under 50 degrees Fahrenheit, they'll need some supplemental warmth.

Keep up daytime temperatures in a room, nursery, or shed where your turtle dwells at around 80 to 90 degrees Fahrenheit with a lolling light at around 95 degrees Fahrenheit. Around evening time, temperatures somewhere in the range of 60 and 80 degrees Fahrenheit are regularly fine. Try not to let the fence in area get excessively cold or your turtle may quit eating and be more vulnerable to ailment.

Light

Turtles housed in an outside nook needn't bother with any exceptional light past the sun. However, when they're housed inside, an UVA/UVB light is important for your sulcata turtle since it won't get normal, unfiltered daylight. The light will enable your turtle to develop solid bones, keep away from malady, and remain sound. Make certain to put the light close enough to your turtle for it to get the advantages, adhering to the item guidelines.

Mugginess

Sulcata turtles favor a mugginess level of around 40 to 55 percent. Mugginess that is too high can prompt contagious contaminations and other issues.1 If you have to raise the stickiness, daintily fog the turtle's walled in area on more than one occasion per day.

Food and Water

Sulcata turtles are herbivorous, touching turtles that need a high-fiber, low-protein diet. This can be given by taking care of an assortment of grasses and feeds (containing at any rate 75 percent of their eating routine), alongside some consumable weeds and blossoms, for example, dandelions, clover, endive, and desert flora cushions. Limited quantities of other verdant green vegetables are likewise fine. But dodge or stay away from nourishments high in oxalates, for example, spinach, mustard and beet greens, kale, broccoli and cauliflower.

Your turtle will snack on the grasses and weeds in its condition for the duration of the day, and you should offer a serving of mixed greens of other verdant greens and vegetables each one to two days. Check with your veterinarian to ensure you're offering the best possible assortment and amount, as this to a great extent relies upon age, size, and wellbeing.

Numerous proprietors supplement the veggies with a calcium and nutrient or vitamin D3 powder a few times per week (or as directed).Do not take care of your pets with natural products, creature protein, or pelleted turtle nourishments from the pet store except if coordinated by your veterinarian. The turtles get a large portion of their hydration from their food; however you likewise ought to incorporate a shallow water dish in their walled area that you invigorate day by day.

CHAPTER THREE

PICKING YOUR SULCATA TORTOISE AS WELL AS SOME HEALTH CHALLENGES OF SULCATA TORTOISE YOU SHOULD KNOW

A sulcata turtle from a trustworthy raiser who can educate you regarding its wellbeing history is urgent. This is a creature you'll apparently have for quite a while, so you'll need to begin a sound foot. Reproducers are genuinely simple to discover over the United States because of the creature's ubiquity. Hope to pay somewhere in the range of $50 and $200 on normal ground for a youthful sulcata turtle.

Search for a turtle with clear eyes and a smooth shell. Also, if conceivable, request to see it eat. A sound sulcata turtle is an unquenchable eater; if it's not taking food, this could be an indication of ailment. In particular, be certain you're capable of embracing such a huge creature that could hypothetically outlast you. Numerous sulcata turtles are sadly re-homed. So you'll have to have an arrangement set up for somebody to think about your turtle in case you'll be busy.

Normal Health and Behavior Problems

In the same way as other reptiles, sulcata turtles are inclined to respiratory contaminations, particularly on the off chance that they're kept in situations that are excessively moist. Furthermore, as different turtles and turtles, shell decay is a typical issue. This is typically brought about by a parasitic disease that prompts a flaky, dry shell.

Metabolic bone infection is another genuine infirmity among turtles and other reptiles. When the creature's phosphorous-to-calcium proportion is out of parity, it can prompt relaxing and debilitating of its bones. This illness can cause deformations and inevitably demise if not treated appropriately.

These conditions are treatable by a veterinarian who has practical experience in reptiles provided they are informed earlier enough. Try not to attempt to treat your turtle with home cures except if suggested by your vet.

CHAPTER FOUR

SULCATA TORTOISES AS GOOD PETS, PLUS PROS & CONS YOU SHOULD KNOW

Sulcatas are known to be truly amiable with their proprietors. They can shape associations with their proprietor, remember them and have remarkable characters.

The Sulcata is an inquisitive and resigned turtle that makes an extraordinary pet – in any event, for family units with small kids.

In the event that you live some place warm and have an enormous yard, at that point this species is an ideal decision for you.

Some facts:

-Generally simple to think about once their nook is constructed.

-A long life expectancy which implies they will be with you forever.

-Cordial and individual characters.

Cons

Tunneling practices can prompt heaps of harm in your yard.

Monster size requires a ton of room to meander and touch.

Need hot temperatures and a luxuriating spot more noteworthy than 100 degrees.

Species Appearance

Sulcata Tortoise Shell

The Sulcata Tortoise's yellowish skin
and tan to brown shell make them
simple to spot! It likewise causes them
cover in their local sandy desert
condition.

Their other regular name, the African
Spurred Tortoise, is a result of the a few
prods situated on their thighs. They
likewise have exceptionally
unmistakable covering and huge scopes
on their front and back legs.

The head of their shell is oval fit as a
fiddle and has a few all around
characterized grooves. Their scutes are
lighter in the center and plot by an a lot
more obscure earthy colored shading.

When these turtles arrive at 15 pounds, it is conceivable to recognize guys from females:

The base of guys' shells (for example plastron) is bended inwards versus females that are level.

Guys create butt-centric scutes that are "V" fit as a fiddle and females create "U" formed scutes.

Guys have longer tails than females.

Albeit some are somewhat lighter, and others hazier, most Sulcatas have a similar run of the mill yellow, tan, and earthy colored shading. Nonetheless, there are ivory and pale skinned person transforms that are a lot lighter in shading.

How Big Do Sulcata Tortoises Grow up?

Infant Sulcatas are conceived at around two crawls in size. Their development rate will fluctuate extraordinarily dependent on their eating regimen, fenced area, and condition.

Solid turtles will arrive at seven crawls at one year old and addition five to ten pounds every year.

They are extremely moderate cultivators and won't arrive at their grown-up size until 15 to 20 years of age.

Grown-up females will normally gauge 70 to 90 pounds and measure 24 to 30 inches. Guys will be somewhat bigger than females.

Probably the biggest and most seasoned Sulcatas have arrived at loads a lot more prominent than 100 pounds.

CHAPTER FIVE

MORE ON SULCATA TORTOISE MEALS, SIGNS OF INFECTIONS IN THEM PLUS OTHER FACTS

Sulcata Tortoise Diet as well as Food Guide

This turtle is an herbivore. In the wild, they in an assortment of grasses and different plants. This eating routine ought to be taken care of in bondage. In a perfect world, they ought to get a wide range of sorts of greens.

Various blossoms can be utilized to change up their eating routine:

-Spring blends.

-Kale.

-Collard greens and turnip greens.

-Mulberry leaves and grape leaves.

-Plantation grass roughage.

-Most garden grasses.

In any event 80% of their every day admission ought to be from the greens and grasses referenced previously. Products of the soil ought not be a significant part of a sulcata turtle's food admission. Pumpkin and watermelon skins are a decent incidental treat.

More seasoned Sulcatas will go through the majority of their day touching in the yard. It is significant not to treat your garden with pesticides or composts as they can be poisonous to turtles.

Their eating regimen can be enhanced with business pellets, anyway the greater part of their sustenance should originate from new greens and grass.

Calcium is a significant supplement that can coincidentally be disregarded by learners.

In the wild, these turtles get calcium from roots, soil, bone pieces, and snail shells.

In imprisonment you can either give them a calcium supplement or cuttlefish bones. In the event that you decide to give them a calcium supplement, use it a few times each week and ensure it doesn't have nutrient or vitaminD3 – an excess of can be harmful.

As a reptile that flourishes in the desert their water admission isn't high. To guarantee they get a satisfactory measure of water, you can douse their day by day greens for a couple of moments before taking care of them.

A shallow water bowl can likewise be given however ought to be cleaned regularly as they will in general poop in it.

At last, it is essential to absorb your turtle shallow warm water two times each week for in any event say 15 minutes and to keep their skin solid.

This species is an exceptionally tough reptile that flourishes in the cruel states of a desert. In any case, there are a couple of medical problems that they face in bondage if not appropriately housed or took care of a right eating regimen:

Taking care of a high protein diet or keeping stickiness levels excessively low in their fenced in area can cause a pyramiding of their scutes.

They are inclined to diseases from sodden and dismissed substrate. These diseases ordinarily present themselves as white patches on their skin or shell and are typically connected with a foul smell.

Lack of hydration is a typical medical problem. It is typically connected with weight reduction, torpidity, flaky skin, and dry dung. Hatchlings are incredibly inclined to lack of hydration as they have exceptionally slim skin and can dry out rapidly.

Metabolic bone infection is likewise normal in turtles that are not housed or taken care of accurately. Sulcatas not took care of enough calcium or nutrient D or not gave enough UVB light will create shell anomalies.

Other potential medical problems in bondage are respiratory diseases, egg authoritative and bladder stones.

Most medical problems are related with a lessening in action and weight reduction.

You ought to normally screen your pet's weight, and on the off chance that it begins to decrease anytime, it is ideal to talk with a vet.

Signs They Are Healthy

-Uniform shell liberated from trash, chips, and anomalies.

-Great craving and action.

-Mouth, nose, eyes, and ears clear without any indications of release or aggravation.

-All around framed and firm defecation and white urates.

Infection Symptoms

-Mouth breathing or hanging of the head.

-Weight reduction and dormancy.

-Watery defecation.

-Release from the mouth, nose, eyes, or ears.

Sulcata Tortoise Enclosure

Sulcata Tortoises are found in the deserts and fields of northern Africa.

In the wild they use tunneling as an approach to get away from the warmth and to assimilate water. Numerous other desert species will assume control over their tunnels to likewise get away from the extraordinary temperatures.

Their caves can arrive at profundities of up to 10 feet.

The thickness of the dirt is critical to their regular practices. In the event that the dirt is excessively firm they can't tunnel and if the dirt is too free their tunnels self-destruct.

They ought to be housed inside until they are sufficiently huge to get away from predators.

After they arrive at two years old or eight creeps in size they ought to be moved to an outside pen with heaps of soil to complete their regular tunneling practices and has enough space to brush.

While moving them outside, it is critical to incorporate an all around protected concealing box to help with homeostasis and with evading predators.

Walled area Type: open air (More Explanation

Size: 100 square feet with 12-inch dividers.

Lighting: UVB lighting (whenever housed inside).

Bedding: Eco earth and sand.

In spite of the fact that this turtle develops gradually, it is ideal to begin with an extremely enormous tank as they will at present grow out of littler tanks generally quick.

A 50-gallon glass tank is suggested for their first year. Plastic tubs and turtle tables are likewise reasonable.

After their first year, they should move to an outside nook.

An open air nook ought to be at any rate 100 square feet and have dividers that are at any rate two feet tall and one foot down. Sulcatas are very solid so the dividers must be safely fabricated. You can utilize cinderblocks to improve the divider's soundness.

Sulcata turtles are enthusiastic climbers so their walled in area ought to have logs, rocks, and different highlights for them to scale. Concealing spots ought to likewise be added to their cave.

A shallow water dish is another adequate expansion.

Since they start from hot parched atmospheres, moistening isn't suggested. You ought to anyway give a shallow drenching dish or absorb them shallow water in any event two times every week.

Lighting and Heating (More Explanation)

As ectotherms, turtles control their internal heat level through their condition. Turtles require UVB light to deal with calcium and produce nutrient D3.

In the event that they are housed outside they will get their required UVB from direct daylight.

For indoor fence in areas you will require an UVB light source. Since they likewise need a luxuriating bulb it is conceivable to purchase lights that produce both warmth and UVB beams. You can buy a hood for the walled in area that can hold the essential lolling and UVB bulbs.

Sulcata Tortoises need a daytime temperature of between 85 to 95 degrees and a relaxing spot more prominent than 100 degrees.

Keeping up the right mugginess level is important to help keep your reptile hydrated and to keep up solid skin.

They need a mugginess of 40% to 60% with hatchlings expecting nearer to 60%. A hygrometer ought to be utilized to screen moistness.

Sulcata Tortoise Bedding

A blend of earth and sand is favored for an infant Sulcata when housed inside. There are some different substrates that will do the trick on the off chance that you can't acquire that blend: cypress mulch, aspen mulch, and orchid bark.

Their substrate ought to be changed week after week and their walled in area ought to be cleaned with cleanser and warm water at any rate once per month.

When lodging them outside ensure they have a lot of non-harmful grass to nibble and soil to cover them in.

Clean their pen of dung and food scraps every day.

Sulcatas have two fundamental exercises they invest a large portion of their energy doing relying upon the season:

Tunneling

At the point when temperatures are cooler they will touch for quite a long time in light of the fact that their huge size requires a ton of calories.

As temperatures become more sweltering and friendlier they will burrow broad tunnels to escape the sun. Strangely they likewise rub their spit on their arms to help chill them off.

Sulcata turtles will spend their mornings luxuriating in the sun to raise their internal heat levels after a cool night.

In the wild they are especially forceful towards one another. They will endeavor to flip each other over and guys will slam to show strength. Females will in general be less forceful however can even now give indications of animosity. Consequently, it is ideal to house them independently.

Turtles utilize a few types of correspondence, for example, vocalization, physical developments, and pheromones. They likewise utilize their mouth and feet to investigate various highlights of their condition through taste and contact.

In contrast to different turtles and turtles, the Sulcata doesn't rest in nature. Nonetheless, they may incidentally enter brief times of brumination in bondage.

Dealing with Vital Advice and Tips

The Sulcata Tortoise loathes dealing with.

Hatchling and adolescents get worried during dealing with and grown-ups regularly become too hefty to even consider lifting!

In the event that you do need to deal with your Sulcata, at that point don't stick or limit it. Move it gradually, be controlled, and don't lift them extremely far over the ground.

Wash your hands when taking care of to forestall communicating microorganisms.

More Facts on Sulcata Tortoise

It is conceivable to discover them for nothing from individuals looking to re-home. Since they are exceptionally well known, and have life expectancies of more than 100 years, there are numerous turtles accessible for re-homing.

You ought to play out a full physical test on any turtle before selection:

Check its nose, eyes, ears, and mouth for release

Check its shell for abnormalities or disfigurements

They ought to likewise be brilliant, alarm, and dynamic.

Guys start mating with females by enclosing them and smashing. Females lay around 20 eggs and cover them 10 inches down. It takes around eight months before the eggs will bring forth.

Sulcata tortoises can cause incredible pets if proprietors to do their examination before receiving.

They need a ton of room to touch and do best in hotter more dry atmospheres. You should construct a huge open air walled area with a lot of concealing spots and deterrents for your turtle to climb and stock up on grasses.

Their broad life expectancy, appealing character, and capacity to be housed outside, lures proprietors everywhere on over the world to get them.

They can frame solid associations with their proprietors and are one of the most fascinating turtles with regards to imprisonment. Happy turtle raising!

THE END

Printed in Great Britain
by Amazon

55687855R00031